Mother/Land

Abenaki poet, CHERYL SAVAGEAU has been awarded Fellowships in
Poetry from the National Endowment for the Arts and the
Massachusetts Artists Foundation, and three residencies at the
MacDowell Colony. Her second book of poetry, Dirt Road Home, was a
finalist for the Paterson Poetry Prize. She was awarded Mentor of the
Year by Wordcraft Circle of Native Writers and Storytellers, as well as
Writer of the Year for her children's book, Muskrat Will Be Swimming.
Savageau also works as a textile artist. Her quilts have recently been
exhibited at the University of New Hampshire in Durham.

Mother/Land

Cheryl Savageau

SALT

Cambridge

PUBLISHED BY SALT PUBLISHING
PO Box 937, Great Wilbraham. Cambridge PDO CB1 5JX United Kingdom
PO Box 202, Applecross, Western Australia 6153

First published 2006

Printed and bound in the United Kingdom by Lightning Source

Typeset in Swift 9.5/13

ISBN-13 978 1 84471 269 4 paperback
ISBN-10 1 84471 269 9 paperback

TB

1 3 5 7 9 8 6 4 2

To Bill

it's good where we've been and where we're going

Table of Contents

Acknowledgments

Mother/Land was written during the most reclusive time in my life. But no matter how much I seem to be hibernating underground, there is always the network of relations without whom no work would ever be accomplished. For those who fed me, nourished me with meals and conversation, put up with me through the darkest times, I thank you from my heart. To Lisa Brooks, *nerdobasqua par excellence,* for porch-sitting, blues-singing, for believing in the poems and the vision, for your insights into history and language, for invaluable help in merging two manuscripts into one book, *wliwni.* To Siobhan Senier, for refusing to let the bear hibernate, for your good humor in learning how to visit Abenaki-style, for your continual encouragement and support and for getting the word out there, many thanks. To Adelle Leiblein, who saw the first drafts of so many of these poems, and who challenges me always to go deeper, many thanks. To Diane Hebert, who was there at the beginning, for inspiration, late-night questions from cyberspace, and for early readings of the mother poems, thank you. To Craig Womack, for writing that makes me have to get up and move, for your stories, for Hank Williams, *wliwini nidoba.* Thanks to all the poets of River Rising. To Lisa Clark and her family, many thanks. To Neil Salisbury, for encouraging the first poems in the "unhistory," thank you. To Dick Wilkie, for his enthusiasm for my work and deep appreciation of spirit of place, and for being an oasis in the desert of graduate school, many thanks. To my children and grandchildren, Chris, Marci, Joe, and Adam, who deepen my life in so many ways, such joy I thought I wouldn't know in this life, love and thanks. To my mother, Cecile, this is the gift I give back. With great thanks to the beautiful land of Ndakinna, to the ancestors, to all my relations, *wliwini.*

Mother/Land

The First Diamond

this
is the place
where time
slows down, where
light is collected and flashes
in all the colors of love it is
the eternal place where she meets him
in the heat of desire and the pressure
of clasped bodies here they turn
the opaque dark
into radiant
seed

Amber Necklace

inspired by ants
I tasted the sap
that oozed in great drops
from the bark of the pine
it tasted like its needles smelled
like winter like mountains or early morning
too strong for more than just a taste too sticky
to roll into the ball I wanted to carry in my hands like
a golden marble. I worried for the tree
was it hurt? I asked *no just leaking* my father told me
it's made so much extra food
he told me how even in deepest winter
you will not starve in a pine grove
how there is always food within
how the sweet globules turned over millions of years
hard as stone how the insects were caught inside
preserved forever
it is not the insects I want but the sweetness they signify
I am caught in the sweet amber
of my mother's hair
nourished
by the light and dark of her
yes and the sticky
the too hard to manage
the I can't get it
off my hands
I want it now
those moments
of petrified love
where we first find ourselves
caught
before we know
what will preserve us

Turtle

this little emerald is dark and shy
does not proclaim itself
with bright lights but swims through
far away stars twinkling near dawn
you may not see it at first think
only darkness but its heart is green

The Moon's Other Face

these are the shadow
footsteps the mysterious
path where flowers grow
in shades of lavender
and lilac deep rose and
indigo their edges limned
in ghostlight this
is the place of secrets the place
women go where men
can't follow the soft
darkness the safe
night

these luminous leaves
come from the moon's garden
I know she has walked there
more than once, her skin
pale her face round
and radiant
in the morning
she dipped the edges
in sunlight watched the ribs
fill with gold
when she
wears them now
they flutter in moonlight
no one can take
their eyes
from her face

First Woman

It is because
she feels like this

sun on morning dew
a drop of water on her heel

white butter
gritty

against the teeth
like corn in august

roasted in sea salt
and sand

Opals

how I loved this ring
the pink fire in the blue
this ring my mother chose
in celebration of her first pregnancy
from a box presented to her at dinner
by my father's boss

choose whatever you want
he said, and she chose
my father's birthstone
the stone that shone like
fire in a blue sky

five round opals, the largest in the center
set in a row in gold, the setting like lips, like
an open mouth, like a woman giving
birth to the child, and the dreams

Game Bag

. . . for Joe Bruchac

Grandmother Woodchuck

This grandson of mine always has a better idea. Why not capture
all the animals in one huge bag, he thinks to himself. Why not tie
up the eagle who creates the wind? And no sooner does he think
it, than he does it. Still, that is the way he learns. Someday he will
grow up. People will speak well of him. Doesn't he always listen to
his grandmother in the end?

Gifts

Grandmother Woodchuck pulls the hair from her belly, from the
tender place. Each pull stings. But she will do this for the grand-
son who will bring tobacco back for her in her old age. She
weaves the hair into a game bag, one that will stretch big enough
to hold all the animals in the world. It is a woman's strength that
will hold them, and a woman's strength that will set them free.

Inside

We are a million eyes open in the dark. We are chipmunk and
mole, rabbit and squirrel. We are musk and fur and claw and
feathers. We are fox, raccoon, mink, and fisher. We are chick-
adees, blue jays, owls, and turkeys. We are hooves and hide, deer
and elk, moose and caribou. Lynx and bear, cougar and wolf. We
are all listening in the dark for the sound of the world ending.

The Conversation

— Why are you always doing things like this?

— It seemed like a good idea at the time.

The World Is Restored

When he finally let us out, I thought there'd be nothing left. But here it is, just as before, only more beautiful. Trees, air, water, and the sound of all of us breathing in the dark woods.

Ant Tree

This is the tree that's inhabited. I like all the little doorways, the tunneled world they live in. I travel with them into the dark heart of the tree, through the living wood, tasting the smells, hearing all the tiny feet walking steadily in. When I put a stalk of grass into the hole, ants climb out on the bridge and onto my hand. I put the stalk of grass next to them, along the side of my arm, and they obligingly climb back off. I slip the grass back into a hole in the tree so they can find their way home. Inside somewhere, I know there is a queen, fat with eggs, who smells so good these ants will not go far. I know that feeling, the good smell of my mother, my Memere, the kitchen smells of home.

Emerald

here is the woman of the woods
the green woman
who makes things grow
she is not as easy as you think
she has her rules
break them at your peril
make her angry
and she will make a world
more barren than ice
let her be and she will
cover you with green

Hair

After oatmeal
Memere makes braids
She combs out yesterday's
adventures
drops light brown burrs
and black sticktights
into the bowl
with what's left of the milk
and brown sugar
like some new kind of cereal

She pulls the braids tighter
and burrs roll over my tongue
sticktights cling to the insides
of my cheeks, hang
from the roof of my mouth.
quiet, she says to my complaint,
stay out of the woods.

The Willow at Flint Pond

. . . . for Denise

Under the willow is where my sister and I spend the afternoon, hot in our pink and blue raincoats, while we wait for the newspapers to be delivered and the rain pours down. The air is warm and smells like places far away. I like the way it touches my cheeks, like my mother's hand the way I want it to be, soft and delicate, with the scent of roses and rain. We watch as the water collects into little streams and runs down the banking into the pond behind the willow, its edges thick in cattails ripe with fluff, carrying sticks, paper ice cream wrappers, bits of bark. Soon we are helping things along, giving things a push, blocking the water with our feet til it runs over our rubber boots. There's still no papers. The wind is blowing hard, but it's not cold. The willow bends her arms low around us, so we don't see our father when he drives by, looking for us. The wind blows our names places we can't hear. After a while, no more cars go by on the cut-off, there is just us, the wind heavy with dark and damp, as we wait under the willow.

At Sugarloaf, 1996

. . . . for Marge

i. *Ktsi Amiskw*

In the big pond, Ktsi Amiskw, the Beaver, is swimming. He has built a dam. The water in his pond grows deeper. He patrols the edges, chasing everyone away. This is all mine, he says. The people and animals grow thirsty.

Cut it out, Creator says. And turns Ktsi Amiskw to stone. The pond is drained. There is water and food for everyone. See those hills, Ktsi Amiskw's head, body, and tail? He's lying there still, this valley his empty pond.

ii. *Ktsi Amiskw Dreams*

For living out of balance, Ktsi Amiskw lies still, while for centuries, his descendants are trapped in every stream, caught in every river, killed by the millions for fur-lust from across the sea. Their pelts buy blankets, cloth, weapons, knives.

In this world out of balance, Ktsi Amiskw dreams a hard dream: a world without beavers. Then, far away, like the promise of a winter dawn, he dreams the rivers back, young mothers building, secure in their skins, and a pond full of the slapping tails of children.

Fertility Figure

this silvery metal snake
  she wore around her arm
    before I was born perhaps
        she imagined herself
      Cleopatra, as I did,
    trying it on as a child
is it an asp? is it
    a cobra unhooded? in
      Greece, the snake brings
        fertility, the women
          feed them milk
    maybe she'd heard about that
    because sometime
after my first brother
    was born and the doctor
      warned her against
        further pregnancies,
          her life at risk, after
          rhythm roulette and the
        visits to priests and
      finally the bishop
who counselled her
    to live with my father
      "as brother and sister"
        rather than commit the
        sin of lust, she stopped
    wearing the snake, still, she
welcomed each new life,
    but I remember she
  shrieked when my
    brothers brought a
      snake into the house
      she, who used to
    love the cold
  wriggling next to
    her skin

Twentieth Anniversary Diamond

she is in the hospital
having their sixth child
another April baby
the month of diamonds
she has told my father
already that she wants a big
ring, a showy ring
and the man-made diamonds
are real really honey
don't spend money
we don't have
when he brings her the ring
the light on their faces
is bright over the newborn
the stone is large on her hand
the jewel
is in her arms

Algonkian Paradise

It would be hard to starve here. The rivers and lakes are full of fish, the coast lavish with shellfish, the forest full of game. Bears, deer, caribou and moose. Rabbits, beavers, squirrels, turkeys, partridge, doves. The trees are full in their season with acorns and nuts. Every place you turn, there is food. The ponds with their cattails, water lilies, sweetflag, the fields with sunflowers, groundnuts, and sweet berries of every kind—strawberries, blue-berries, red and black raspberries, blackberries, cranberries, grapes, sumac, mayapple. And the great maples full of sweet sap. The missionary Pierre Biard complained, "Abundant plant, animal, fish, and shellfish resources provided the Algonkian a lavish living, all without work." A condition he felt, that should only be found in Paradise.

Had he ever gone fishing for the elusive food? Gathered nuts, or berries deep in thorns and mosquitoes? Ever tracked a deer through snow, skinned a rabbit, pounded dried berries into smoked meat? Rendered bear fat, thrust hands deep into the mud to harvest the roots of cattails? Dug clams, gathered mussels in cold wind or burning sun? Tanned hides, made a canoe, designed and crafted snowshoes for the whole family?

My father told me that Creator gave us the most beautiful place on the planet to live, and I won't dispute that. And if we could have the land back the way it was, it would be Paradise, for sure.

And don't we love the feel of ash splitting perfectly in our hands . . .

Race Point, Provincetown

is where I first see
the spouting far out
in the steel sea
my father inhales smoke
sends it back into the air
in a stream that vanishes
in the sea breeze
it's whale he says
to my unasked question
smoking Gluscap's pipe
my father settles back
with his cigarette
and I watch whale
sending fountains of prayer
skyward with each breath

The Grand Banks

From the ocean's depths,
from the dark place,
rising up from the sea floor,
this great underwater plateau,
this dinner table for fish,
this underwater banquet,
this feasting place where haddock and cod
gather like buffalo, their numbers too great to imagine.
The currents hit the slopes, feeding nutrients from sea bottom,
the water rich with plankton, algae, diatomic life. Whales come
from the warm waters of the south to raise their young here
where food is plentiful, filling the waters with song that can be
heard for a thousand miles, more. Ocean is their word for world.

Pies

so many of them
we had to count each christmas
two apple, a lemon meringue,
chocolate cream with and without
sugar, coconut cream, banana
cream, squash, pineapple,
pecan and of course
the too'kays waiting in the freezer
a dozen or more
enough to last til new year's

vacation meant hunting out a good
blueberry patch, braving mosquitoes
and heat for the sweet jewels
then the september drive to the orchard
where inevitably someone would
fall in poison ivy but oh
the pies! macintosh of course
the sweetest the only
apple according to my mother

we all agreed that no one
could make her crust though
mine comes the closest
it was something in the tender
way she touched the dough
the way she worked
each particle as she rolled
the flour and fat
through her hands
something like
the way a potter
turns the clay
a jeweler
polishes a stone
a poet turns a phrase

Bread

it is the warm white loaves
rising in willow baskets
in your winter kitchen
yellow walls
promising sun

it is the bread
the living breath of it
under my kneading hands
the yeasty smell of it hot off
the stone the round goodness of it
pressed to my face it is the taste
of warm bread I want between my lips
new as a love affair, familiar
as mother's milk
on my tongue

ah, but this is no meal
for an infant, there is garlic
here, onion, scallion and sage,
basil and the memory of olives
basking in hot sun sweet anise
lives in this bread, dark chocolate,
and the scent of espresso drunk
after midnight this bread holds
the briny taste of sea, of shrimp
and salt, butter and lemon, of
honey, almonds and cognac
ah, I could get drunk
on this bread

bring me your blue bowl and wooden spoon
bring me your loaves, warm to the touch
and tender on the tongue,
the sweet yeasty promise
of tomorrow's bread

Where I Want Them

on the lids of my eyes on the nape
of my neck across the top of my
shoulder down the side of my
arm grazing the hair and over the
knuckle of each finger and then
the fingertips one at a time in
the center of my palm on the tender
inside of my forearm in the crease
of my underarm the hollow of my
throat between my breasts circling
each nipple circling my navel following
the line of my backbone to the small
of my back on the mound of each
cheek on the tender underside of my
ass on the backs of my knees on the
inside of my thighs on the lips of the
flower where you will find me
trembling

Swift River—Kancamagus

. . . for Lisa

we pull off the road
to this place
where in summer
swimmers
loll on the rocks
like otters
grandmothers
and grandbabies
wade in the icy
shallows where
sand has been pounded
soft and teenagers
dive into deeper
pools and come
out shining
beaded with water

today it is just us
and we walk out
over the boulders
find one mid-river
and sit, back-to-back

we have just driven
down the Kancamagus
from the high spot
that separates
the watersheds
one flowing east,
the other west and south
the directions of her
people and mine

We laugh to realize
she is facing west
I am facing east
we've done this without
thinking
someday someone will
find two women in rock
back to back
on this mountain
facing sunset, facing dawn

Red

In his new poem
the red autumn woods
are a metaphor
for leftist martyrs
We are traveling east through a maple forest
that blazes the hillsides on both sides of this winding
back-country road Look at the trees I want to tell him
Listen The trees have their own stories to tell
like the story of fire deep within the heart They too
have been martyrs in the long war against the land, a nation
cut down, children denied
A hundred years ago these hills were bare of trees
the stone walls that wind through them
the illusion of ownership Now the hills are red with maples
My heart is leaping out to meet them, my eyes
cannot be full enough Though acid falls from the clouds
maples have gathered on the hillsides
in every direction See how they celebrate
They are wearing their brightest dresses
Come sisters, let me dance with you
I offer you a song
Let me paint
it red with
passion
You are
all the women
I have ever loved

. . . for Chrystos

Ghosts
At the Center
of the World

Garnet

this is the mother's heart
the deepest red this is where roses
grow in greatest profusion each one covering
a thorn red roses of blood white roses of milk
this is the heart of sorrow of birth and sustenance
and loss of blood that has been shed over and
over again this is the mother's heart
the garden of transformation
where she will give birth
one more time
and know herself
as love

Hummingbird Moth

"... *did you ever try to catch*
a hummingbird in your hands?"
—Maurice Kenny

there's a hummingbird in the refrigerator
there's a hummingbird in the refrigerator?
or maybe it's a moth
there's a hummingbird in the refrigerator?

did you ever try to catch
a hummingbird in your hands?

each morning
my mother watered
the geraniums she grew
especially for the hummingbirds
and one day her green eyes
were caught
by flickering wings
feathery tufts
a glittering
something
she

clapped

between her hands
do insects have feathers?
she asks me

I saved it for you
it's in the fridge

there's a hummingbird in the refrigerator
or maybe it's a moth
whatever it is
it's in the fridge

before opening the door
my brother says
it's probably
the last of its kind

Cod

It is the fish that bring them first.
Cod in such numbers as to seem endless.
Cod to fill the nets and bellies of hungry
Europeans with the tender white flesh.
Cod, it seems to them, without end.

They fill the ships,
salting the fish
down in barrels,
til the hull is full,
and head back home. This wet
cod-fishing goes on for
years, far out in the Banks,
with only an occasional stop on land.

We dry our fish in the sun
cure it in smoke-houses
and sure enough, the
foreigners hear
about it.

Soon they need
a land base
to dry the cod
which weighs less
than when wet
tastes better, too

it is these dreams
of cod that
first bring
the French
to land

dreams
of cod
the gold
of the sea
that will
fill their bellies
and their
pockets

Everywhere

Suddenly
they are everywhere

They circle like vultures
but they are not vultures
for they kill their prey

They circle like eagles
but they are not eagles
for they take their prey
not one at a time
but by the thousands

They cast nets like spiders
but they are not spiders
for they have forgotten
the strands of connection

They look like human beings
but they leave no gifts
and the songs they sing
are only for themselves

Before Moving on to Plymouth
from Cape Cod—1620

. . . for Donna and John

they find what looks like
a grave
what looks like a grave
a grave and they
dig it up
they find a grave
it looks like
a grave
and they dig
it up
they dig it up the grave
it looks like they
dig it up and
they dig it up and
it looks like
a grave and
they
dig it up

Grandmother Woodchuck Talks to the Women of Salem

You weren't dancing with the devil
when you traveled beneath the moon
and into the trees
but they got it right
when they said
I am covered with hair

You scratched on the door softly
brought me gifts of bacon and black
honey. I taught you how to take
only what you need, to leave
the mother plant behind.
I showed you willow bark
for fevers, comfrey for sprains

some of you listened
some of you left afraid
but someone must have told
about the wild yam
that stops the man's seed
or the herbs that release
the unborn child or maybe
it was the songs you sang
as you worked, your hair
worn long and free, or
the words you spoke
which seemed to them
an evil mumbling

they were afraid of us already
afraid of the land they'd stolen
the disease they'd spread
every tree, they said
became an Indian

it didn't take them long
to set the forests tumbling
to hunt away the deer
and kill the wolves
I have seen them

give blankets of death
with smiles that bared
their teeth

Englishmen's Footprints

plantain makes a
good tea. its seeds are
crushed and used as a
laxative. it is found in
every english garden. now
its leaves are pushing up
everywhere. you can find it
outside every english
settlement, its long leaves
with parallel veins,
its central stocks of tiny
flowers. wherever
the english go
plantain
grows in their footsteps.
when you see it
you'll know that they're
near. that english boy
found his way home
following those
footsteps. when
you see it
go the other way

Newfoundland
Walking with Joseph Brant

He is a good man
though like all men
he doesn't stop often enough
to smell the trees and
melting snow

on the island, they are all dead
the pups drowned
the old ones shot
they say some escaped
in boats

I jumped into the sea
saving myself at least
this time
no one knows I'm here
walking these inland woods
where rabbits are plump
and pups won't drown

Daughters of the King

Les Filles du Roi (1668)

French men are marrying Indian women. It will have to be
stopped. Wives will have to be found. French wives for French
men. And so the call goes out to all the unfortunates in France.
Women without homes, without family, poor women, women
alone. Women with no dowries to buy a husband. Become a Fille
du Roi, a Daughter of the King. Each woman considers her
options. The hardships she doesn't know are preferable to the
ones she knows too well. As a Daughter of the King, she will have
a dowry, payable to her husband at the time of marriage. She will
have a home, the possibility of children, a place in the
community. Women come from Ile de France, from Normandy,
800 women in ten years. Les Filles du Roi.

Une Fille du Roi—Marie Mazol, 1668

Marie Mazol is thirty three years old when she becomes a
Daughter of the King. She will bring 300 livres to her marriage to
Antoine Roy-Desjardins. She will have money for her own use as
well, for expenses, they promise her. She thought it would go
further, but what she takes with her are a coffer, a cap, a taffeta
handkerchief, a shoe ribbon, a hundred needles, a comb, a pair of
stockings, a pair of gloves, a pair of scissors, two knives, a
thousand pins, a bonnet, and four laces. Thus prepared, she faces
marriage to a man she doesn't know, in a country she's never
seen.

Les Filles du Roi—Afterwards

The Daughters of the King become wives. But French and Indian
keep marrying. Their descendants will say, "Scratch a Frenchman,
find an Indian."

Mendel's Milkmen

we are all in the car
with our various colored hair
me a bottled blond this first
year of high school, my
sister brunette, one brother
red-haired, and the two
babies different shades
of brown, when two
nuns come running over
for a ride to the dentist.
it is our first year
of catholic schools and
nuns are still a novelty
they climb into the car
and maybe overwhelmed
by sheer numbers exclaim
my, your children all look so
different!
they do not know my
father, black-haired
hazel-eyed, nor
apparently
the wily ways
of genetics.
I roll my eyes
having already heard
of Mendel, and how
a great-grandfather's
eyes can lay hidden for
generations then
flash in a newborn's face
the incongruity of
blonds with dark skin
and I know how the
ancestors come back

my mother
just raises her eyebrows
turns the wheel
and steps on the gas
and without missing a beat says
different milkmen, sisters,
different milkmen

Pink Sapphire

it is a delicacy I don't show the world
more suited to my willowy niece, the curly
red-haired double to my mother

I don't remember my mother wearing this ring
It is the secret child, not the playful one
who tap dances, leads parades of children
around the park with an imaginary baton
runs with a kite on windless days
while my brothers shout, *Run, Ma, Run*

No, not that child, this ring, but the other one
shy, ashamed of her red hair and freckles,
helping her mother bring in the groceries,
praying novenas beside her in church
for the health and sobriety of her father

She is the one I understood, the girl without
a childhood, the delicate rose dreaming
through the harsh season

The Kneeling Girl

always before
it was madonnas
in gold frames
on the wall

now it is
the kneeling girl
on the coffee table

it is the lotus
she wants
to fill the vessel of stars
offered by the kneeling girl
somewhere in this lotus
is the jewel

Mexican Amethyst

she and my father
chose the stone
and watched the artisan
fashion the gold

my father, a welder once
in the South Pacific
braided a ring
of gunmetal
sent it home to his mother
wear it til I get home
he wrote her
and she did
she told me the story herself
and wore it til her death
when it came to me

he watches now
my father
with a craftsman's interest
how the metal responds
bending and curving
in the heat
how the jeweler
coaxes the gold
into a braided circle
sets the stone
in place

for my mother
it is a flower being born

someone's hands loved this gold
this purple stone, flawed,
humble in its gold casing
a mother I can love

Pearl Cuffs

woven together these thick bands
stretch to go over the hands
make the bare arms exotic
part of a costume

like something a bunny would wear
or a cash girl in Las Vegas or
a dancer in a black sleeveless
leotard with
tophat and cane

Nesting

when I ascend
the altar steps
dressed in white
there is whispering
they notice the new
fullness to my breasts
and wonder
yes
beneath this wide skirt
is the nest I am building
and the egg that has quickened

nobody notices
the knife in my teeth

No Pity

. . . for Awiakta

At breakfast I am rock hard with milk
and the child, eight days out of my body,
and full of his own life, is hungry. I cup my hand
under my breast, to guide it to his searching mouth
and milk sprays out over the breakfast table.

    I am laughing out loud at the wonder of it
    I am Hera spraying stars across the sky
    I am Selu running her hands up her belly
    coaxing waterfalls of corn from her breasts,
    filling baskets

        But he is not laughing,
this young man I call husband. He pushes his
plate away, unable to eat. I have
put him off his breakfast, he says

I am raining blood and milk,
the life of his son, when he tells me,
women are disgusting, they're always
dripping from somewhere.

The marriage ends here,
although he doesn't know it yet,
and continues his pronouncements
for another year or more.

        Women are clever
but not intelligent, he says, emotional
but not passionate.

    He is outside
    and afraid, and I have
    no pity.

Beauty Tip

Women are beautiful
only when perfectly still
he tells me,
quoting Michelangelo
from his chair
while I vacuum the rug

Surrogate Mother

No baby ever
floated in a sea of dreams
inside this wire cage
where no heart beats
but a clock tick tocks
a lie of life
There is no blood
warming the terry cloth skin
no breasts to nourish
no eyes, no fingers
to touch and hold

Still the monkey child clings
to this mother
this surrogate of metal and cloth

I am a woman
The promise I carry
inside the bowl of my body
I nourish with my own blood
I build from the power
of my own flesh
a new body, a child
whose limbs kick
inside the cage of my ribs,
whose head rests
in the rolling boat
of walking hips
whose heart and blood
move with the rhythm
of my own
And when the time is right
it is my body that opens
that is the door into life

My breasts are full of milk
yet this will name me surrogate:
a man with money, a dropperful of semen,
and a wife whose body will not bear.

For Lenny, For Lisa

He is no longer
a young man
he is forty
dead drunk
face down in the pond

All three of his
wives have left him
he's left every
job he's had
every gd boss
who had it in for him

he's tired
he's floating
he's sick
of being jazzed up
and down dirty
and disgusted
all at the same time

he needs a smoke
he needs a sweat
he needs to breathe
but he is face down
in the pond
floating
and moving takes
such effort

below him fish
circle like hawks
he sees their wings
spread in the murky
sky below
now he is walking
in jeans and bare-chested
on a road that shines like
mica in stone cliffs

below him dreams
rise like smoke
from spirit houses
somewhere
his sisters are crying

eagles fly above him now
dropping feathers
each tied to a dream
he follows one back
shows his face
my sister needs this
he tells the dreamer

it is a white man
a colleague
who calls her
into his office

I'm not supposed to
have this he says
as he hands her
the feather
and the dream

her brother
in jeans, bare-chested
continues on the
road he's found
stars shining like mica
in the cliffs of home

The Liar

whatever she says
others must deny
she sees the crack in the cup
the swollen knuckles
she sees the child
who throws the cat
against the wall
the one who destroys
his things in silence
and the one who hides
the ends of sandwiches
under rugs and sofa cushions
she sees the one who
changes moods hourly
like the weather outside
the one who throws
the younger child off the dam
into dark waters
she sees the one who plays
and sings incessantly
the one who is loved
by trees and water
she sees through
the cracks in the stories where
violence flashes in an alcohol
haze she sees the one who gives up
drugs for jesus and the one
who gives up drugs for money
and the one who
gives up everything
for drugs
she sees the one who
hates his mother
for his father's crimes

the one who teases
past all endurance
and the one who hides
from her brother
behind the locked bathroom door
she sees the one who
denies his gifts
the one whose elfin gestures
speak of desires he will not own
she sees the grandmother
who endures everything
and is loved
and dies young
and the one who gives
her drunken husband's
dinner to the dog
and is hated
but endures
she sees love and hate
growing like two vines
through the rooms
of the house
she sees the man
who draws back from his
wide embrace of the world
into the arms of an easy chair
she sees the woman
in underwear and a tight
sweater who shows off her legs
in the tv glow to her husband
and sons, she sees her
buffing the hardwood floors
daily, arranging the pleats

in the curtains, the apples
in the crust according to
some internal plan, she sees
the pattern in booze and blood
and knows it will never
be put right

Aftermath

he is always walking away now
when I see him his head down
so I can't see his face
he has on the suit he wore
in court his dark curly hair
clipped neat for the judge

he is the one I was supposed to
protect
the baby brother I carried
his arms around my neck

who would suspect
his hands?

Rose Quartz Necklace

these rough stones
draw the bewilderment
from her face
stop
her circling
empty her mouth
of the grit
she has swallowed
soon words
will fill her
and after that
song

Tradition

My mother is making apple pie
and I am helping
I am placing the cut slices
into the pie, following
her directions, placing
the half-moons curve side up
along the outer rims,
arranging crescents in circles
from the outside to the center,
flat against the bottom
I cut slices evenly, arrange them in
perfect tiers, leave as little
space between them
as I can manage, til they
mound over the top like a
gentle hill or the
belly of a woman

I can feel her eyes over my shoulder
watching that I do it right
that I've mixed the cinnamon into the
sugar until it's an even brown,
that I've done this before
not after, slicing the apples,
that I pour it over them
in a gently curving spiral
as she's shown me

This is the way it is done

Twenty years later I am helping her again
placing the cut apples
just so, not thinking why

secure in knowing the
right way when she glances over
and asks

why are you doing it like that?

I look at the half moons
running along the outside
crust we've always done it
this way, haven't we? She looks
at me like I am crazy It's the way
you showed me I say I always
do it this way.

          Really, she says
and without ceremony,
dumps the apples into the shell,
spreads them in a heap with her hands
mixes the cinnamon with the sugar
and pours it over the pie
she picks up the pie plate
and shakes it gently
so the sugar settles

I imagine the edges pressed
just so around her thumb
the central steam hole
the knife-slashed arrows
the painting of every
nook and cranny

That's the thing with tradition.
Even now, peeling apples for pie,
I'm looking over my own
shoulder, wondering

Ring of Protection

a single ruby set amidst tiny diamonds
an eye within an eye
fire melts ice
my heart is in my mouth

Poison in the Pond

i.

the skin on my arms burns
It is hot today and sticky
and poison is flowing
out of orange barrels
into the waters of the pond

my eyes burn my lips burn
my tongue is thick
I cannot swallow
my throat is
sore as strep

the fish are dying
turtles wash up on shore
the lilies shrivel
sweetflag blackens
cattails are ragged sticks
the floating island
has stopped wandering

but it is for our own good
they tell us and no one
leaves, we tough it out

those orange barrels
the bans on swimming
on eating fish

our lungs burn
the air is hot and thick

this pond used to want
to be a river
now it wants to be
a meadow

these orange barrels
will teach it who's boss

ii.

the baby is born
wrong there is
something
wrong with the
baby something
is wrong

there are seizures
there is something
about the brain
the parents are
teenagers
did you take drugs
you must've taken drugs

pond water laps the shore
you can see straight
to the bottom

iii.

not everyone is tired
tired when they go to bed
tired when they wake up
too tired to answer the phone
too tired to get dressed too tired
to fix a meal, to take a walk
not everyone is tired
but lots of us are

iv.

it is twenty years
since the poison
barrels floated on flint pond
some of us are in our twenties
some in our thirties
some fifty or older
we ache ache ache we can't
digest our food
we sleep but don't sleep
we push ourselves and crash
we lie in bed and watch tv
don't touch us our skin burns
there are bites from insects
nobody sees water
dripping on shoulders
when there is no rain our feet
run beneath our blankets like
dogs dreaming of the chase
our bones have
turned to sand

v.

it is for your own good
it is all in your mind
it is depression
it is a new disease
it is an old disease only
nobody

knows its name
it is inherited
it is a french-canadian disease
it is a woman's disease
it is all in your head
there's no such thing

vi.

here
take these
little orange pills
it's for
your own good

Smallpox

". . . some of us did not die"
—JUNE JORDAN

i.

it is the animals' revenge
for being held in pens
bred for meat
and docility
we don't have it here

ii.

it is not the big pox
syphilis
which they also
got from sheep
we don't have it here

iii.

there is nothing small
about it
when it comes
the back aches,
the head hurts,
the body burns,
the skin erupts

iv.

as power often does
it comes in four
manifestations

the kind and distinct pox
the confluent
the purples
the bloody pox

it comes in four
manifestations

this does not surprise us

v.

in other places
where women
are healers
the pox has
whispered
secrets
in constantinople
in africa
women search out
the mildest cases
harvest liquid
from the pustules
scratch it lightly
into outstretched
arms

vi.

in boston
in london
people with
scratched arms
live

vii.

none of us
have scratched arms
none of us have
mild cases
we bleed beneath our skin
that sloughs off
our living flesh

viii.

it is some small thing
in us that keeps us
close relatives
some small thing
it is our blood type
it is some allele
some collection of genes
it is in our blood
my relatives

ix.

I have measles
for the second time
it is because I am
indian I know
though no one
will say so
indians don't have
immunity I read it
somewhere lots of them
died will I die
I ask my mother
sleep now
she answers
there is a dark cloth
over the lamp
the light still
hurts my eyes
I am sleeping in her bed
outside the bedroom door
voices mumble
my ears
itch from inside
my skin
is tight and hot

x.

it is after
the bostoniak
doctors learn
to inoculate
it is after
the bostoniak
doctors learn
to vaccinate
it is after
they know how
to prevent it
that they give
the blankets
that will cause it

xi.

there is
no one here
left to take
care of the sick

xii.

some of us
don't die
some of us
don't
some of us
don't die

Indian Blood

My father was
an Indian giver
a universal donor
O negative

O this blood that gives
strength
against the pox
O this blood
that makes my father
proud of phone calls
that come in the middle
of the night
we need your blood
O this blood
that we think
defines us
somehow

O this same blood
that kept a few of us alive
in times of smallpox
O this same blood
that makes us weak
in times of cholera

in the beginning time
the white mountains
rose above the
flood waters
we climbed
to the land of the dead
and watched the
waters recede

the land of the dead
where else
is there to go when
disease
is at every door

O it is here
in the mountains
that the old ones
wait out the
new flood
O what is passed
to their children
besides the stories

O and comes down
to my father
so he can say
yes, I'll come
to the late night calls
he is a universal donor
an Indian giver
a refugee
from the land of the dead

graduate school first semester:
so here I am writing about Indians again

"the conquest is not sustainable . . ."
—Winona LaDuke

thanks for bringing that
to our attention
she said the first time
to my response to a history text
about a famous painting
of the Battle of Quebec
that never mentioned the French
and only mentioned Indians twice,
once as nuisances, once
as the noble savage
kneeling by the dying
English general

this was during
the French and Indian war
I said, soon thousands
of French and Indian people
would be displaced, sold
into indentured servitude
my own family among them
there would be bounties
on the heads of Abenaki people
in Maine, and the English
would sow the fields of the Mohawks
with salt

thanks for bringing that up,
she said

the next book mentioned
cannibals in the Caribbean,
Indians who believed the Spanish were
gods, Indians killing themselves, Indian
women in love with Spanish pricks, Indians
whose names, even when known, were
passed over in favor of the ones
given them by the Spanish

stop writing about
Indians
she told me
you're making everyone
feel guilty

but the next book
was back in Maine
home territory
the diary of a midwife
right after that same
French and Indian war
and she was using herbs
not found in English herbals
and wrote that a "young
squaw" visited her
over a period of
three weeks, but

the famous historian
said only that
there may have been
Indians in the area,
while she wrote

at length about
white men dressing up
as Indians
to protest against the rich
stealing their lands

stop writing about Indians
she told me again
only louder as if
I was hard of hearing
you have to allow authors
their subjects, she said
stop writing about
what isn't in the text

which is just our entire history

this week, she said
I'm really upset
you're telling the same story
three times
because there's only
one story about Indians
and we all know what it is
so I asked her if there are an
infinite number of stories about
white people
and she told me to
stop being racist

so I stayed away from class for a week
because they were reading a book
about a mystery in the Everglades
and I knew there had to be
Indians in that swamp
and I didn't want to have to
write about Indians
again

it was on to the next book
written, she said by
a Cherokee writer,
which Leslie Silko, who is Laguna,
will be interested to find out
because the book was *Ceremony*
but that is a small mistake
sort of like saying that
Dante is Chinese, so
I overlooked it

now, she told me
write about Indians

and I might have done that
except she went on
about Indians putting on
a mask of whiteness
like white people put on
black face, and some of the students
wrote it down in their notebooks
and everyone started talking about
minstrel shows

then she wanted me to tell her
if there is such a thing as
an Indian world view
and I said, well, yes and no,
which I figured was safe
since I would be at least
half-right whichever answer
she wanted, but when I mentioned
the European world view,
she said there isn't any such thing
which was quite a relief to me,
I hate to think there were a
whole lot of people thinking in
hierarchies and as if the
earth is a dead object and
animals and plants and some people
not having spirit
then she said I'd better stick
to what I know, that is,
Indians, which is what
I was trying to do in the first place,
and that maybe European philosophy
was too much for my primitive
brain in spite of its being my
undergraduate major
and I pointed out that the
oppressed always know more
about the oppressor than vice
versa, so she just glared at me
and told me that I look
Scandinavian

which was a surprise to me
and I wondered why I never was a
prom queen since it was always the
Scandinavian girls who got that
honor, maybe they never
noticed I was one of them. Exactly
how much Indian are you anyway?
she asked. I told her I guessed
I was pretty much Indian. I
suppose she wondered
why I wouldn't accept that mask of
whiteness she kept talking about
as myself

Chandelier

after the haggling
over Memere's housedresses
the boxes of handkerchiefs
and cologne still unopened
and finally the tossing of the mattress
for her flattened pocketbooks

after the selling of her house
for less than it was worth
after dividing everything among
the six sisters and one brother
my mother took her part of the
money and ordered it from
a catalogue, a chandelier
with real imported
Austrian crystal

my father, after work
on nights he wasn't going to school
and on weekends
laid walls of cement blocks
for the dining room
with me beside him laying mortar
on the edges as he'd shown me
before he'd lift the block into place
tamp and level it
downing tall glasses of lemonade
my mother sent out
at regular intervals

it took four years before he put up
the faux white ash paneling
laid down the teal carpeting
set the acoustic tile in the ceiling

over the place
where someday a table
would be graced
with holiday dinners
my mother hung her inheritance
set the doily on the card table beneath
arranged the vase of plastic flowers
just so

Crayons

Today I cleaned out my thread box. It's an old tin christmas cookie container with a horse and sleigh on the front. I took out all the spools, rewound the loose threads, and wiped out the dust from the bottom. Then I arranged all the spools on the bed by color. Red, pink, orange, yellow, blue turquoise, purple, brown, black, white. Like crayons in first grade. Or the birthday present I got one year, the crayola in 64 colors. I arranged them over and over again, saying the names—periwinkle blue, burnt sienna, until my younger sister and brothers got ahold of them, and broke them, their small fingers pressing too hard as they drew and colored. My mother took my new box of crayons and dumped them into the big box she'd collected over the years, the one with all the broken crayons, paper stripped off, dusty and dirty, their colors gone dull. I looked at my new crayons in the box, all the broken pieces and cried. My sister and brothers looked sad, but I didn't care, I had to punish them. I hate you, I said. I'll never let you use anything of mine again. I wish I didn't even have a sister or brothers. My mother said I was selfish, that the crayons were just as good broken as whole. Shame on you, she said, for talking to your sister and brothers like that. Someday you'll be alone, she said, and you'll see how it feels. I think of them now as I sort the thread like those old crayons. It has been months since I've seen them, and I want them here. I stack the spools in the tin. If I can just get these spools right. I gather them carefully in, a rainbow I can hold in my hands.

Pink Ice with Marcasite

it is saddle-shaped
with the stone huge and
oval cut it is the reflection of the
Taj Mahal with reflecting pool at sunset
it is two turbaned fortune-tellers
over a glowing ball
a spider spinning
its body faceted pink
its legs covered with dew
it is two women dancing
carrying between them
a drum a pink moon
a light bigger than
both of them

Pemigewasset

we are at the source
the place where the Pemi
streams out of the lake
over the granite
in cascades
and whirlpools

tourists
rush past us
two Abenaki women
gazing silently
into water

I feel like a ghost
she says
they can't even see
us

tourists
follow the signs
to the next
attraction
they don't
want to miss
anything

below us
around us
water is
flowing

that's because
they are in a state park
I say
and we are at
the center
of the world

the rocks
are full of
water
everywhere
water
is moving

Visiting the Land of the Dead

North Country:
Visiting the Land of the Dead

It is colder here and the winds blow more fiercely
than anywhere else
We cross the land of pebbles,
the land of boulders, the land of stones
Pook is pulling, unaccustomed to a leash
My mother walks into air

Entangled

It starts with the stopping of a heartbeat
that explodes into popcorn in my chest
some wild beating out of rhythm

It begins with a dry mouth
a pushing up halfway
from the kitchen table

It begins with a trembling
deep in the blood of arms and legs
a rolling of the eyes

it begins like a gunshot
an arrow a dog's bark
and who can tell the difference

it begins with eyes squinting
against the light, nerves crawling
away from sound and touch

it begins with the smell of a forest
burning on the southern winds

it begins with me tied to you
like entangled atoms

your blood changes
clumps around the rogue protein
swells your joints, clogs
your kidneys
no one, not even you,
knows yet

hours north of you, Mama
I am ready to fight or flee
I am living past the speed
of light, in darkness, spooked
obsessed, quilting furiously

Morning: University Medical Center

beware water the psychic told her

now fluid puffs her cheeks
though today her ankles show a hint
of the slimness she liked to show off in high heels
as she lindy-hopped on Saturday nights

tubes dangle from the catheter
in the vein above her collar bone
where twice daily her blood is
drained through the red line
returned through the blue

IVs and injections have spread
purple bruises like oil spills
across her arms and belly
wires are attached at the EKG points
the monitor dangling to the
hips that held us all those
many months in nurturing fluid

beware water

she wears hospital tan ankle socks
with rubber grips so she won't fall
on her way to the commode
but she is standing firmly today
not wobbling her arms not trembling
as she sweeps the washrag over her breasts
under her arms over her shoulders
and bruised belly between her legs

she does this unself-consciously
I have drawn the curtain around us
and we are alone in this space
looking out over Lake Quinsigamond
I am as naturally tied to her
as a suckling calf
light pours in through the
hospital windows
washes her in morning gold
her red curls disheveled and wild

I hand her towel and robe
she flinches under the comb
this is not something we
do for each other

when I was a girl
all she had to do was pick up
the comb to start me crying
until one day she hit me with the brush
now you'll have something to cry about
she'd said

all these years Mama
I never knew
the world was harsh to you too
your skin too sensitive for touching

I pick up the comb and begin
as if brushing a bird's wing
to smooth the curls.
she relaxes under my hands
Ma, Ma, Mama

Hurricane—North Truro

The beach is full of dune-buggies when we get there. It's from
these dunes that you can see the whales spouting, far off, sending
their breath into the sky. We drive up to my uncle's trailer. It's too
cold to swim here, but we jump into the surf anyway, getting
tangled in strands of seaweed that wraps around our thighs and
gets inside our bathing suits. This is the summer before I get
breasts. My bathing suit is baggy and beginning to disintegrate
from water and sun. My cousin Paula has a waist and hips and
looks good in the black bathing suit that used to be Judy's who's
away at nursing school. A waste of time my uncle says, but I know
she's beautiful and smarter than him, even if he's older. Later we
walk through the dunes. I cut my ankles on witch grass, we
tumble down the sides that are cool and damp away from the
sun. When we get back my father and uncle are getting out of the
boat. The waves behind them are dark green and white, and
getting bigger all the time. My father is carrying a bass, and my
uncle looks likes he's going to puke. He keeps swallowing and
swallowing. My father was in the navy and says these waves aren't
much. Tomorrow all these buggies will go up into the dunes
when the hurricane blows in. My cousins will stay inland with us.
We will sleep in the attic listening to the wind whirling around
the house, closer to us up there under the eaves. We have a
flashlight, and we don't even need ghost stories, the wind is
enough. Hear it? we keep asking each other.

Side Pass

Now my father's eyes are closed
and the boys, now men,
file by giving their hands
to each of us, their eyes
touching our faces
each in turn

For weeks I think of the boy
this first love lost twenty years ago
who shows up at my father's wake
with all the others who called my father
Coach. My curly-haired Italian boy
is this man with diabetes
and bad teeth. I can't

get him off my mind. I am
humming as I iron this blouse
pink like the one he bought me
when I was fifteen. I search
through bureau drawers
for the tiny box that holds
the old necklace, a single pearl
on a white gold chain so thin
it tangles as I lift it from
the tissue paper.

I am crazy
he is married, with a new child,
he doesn't read, I am happy
with my husband, but I am
like a girl waiting for the phone,
I am daydreaming, in love,
I am fifteen

            my father's hands
are holding the ball
in a circle of sweating boys
his eyes are not closed
but on their faces, moths
are circling the lights above
the court, and I am watching
this unlikely team, as he flicks
his wrists

            in a direction he isn't looking
one of them catches the ball, they break
into a run down the court. I am watching
breathless, fifteen

            I would fall in love again
if it would save me from this grief

Night Sky

they address all questions to me
            the eldest, and for a moment
                        I assume the role of matriarch

                        our numbers give us weight
                  her dying gives us gravity
            one could easily think us planets
      and she the star about to go out

I could say her absence is the black hole
            that draws us ever closer into the dense
                        center of love

      we are held in temporary stasis
                  a constellation around her bed
                        soon we will be spiraling
                                    wildly outside her arms

Rosary

not roses
but beads
the color
of a summer sky
not round
but oval
each bead
leading
to the next
a river of
prayer

je vous salue
Marie
pleine de grace

she was five
when she saw
them on display
in the back
of St. Ann's church
where she would make
her first communion
she thought them
the cloak of the Virgin herself
gasped
when her mother took money
from the food allowance
to put the beads
into her hands

Ave Maria
gratia plena
dominus tecum

for sixty-eight years
                the river of beads
                        flowed through her hands
                        each night of her marriage
                she and my father together
        prayed to the Blessed Mother

        hail Mary
                full of grace
                        the lord is with thee
                                blessed art thou
                                        amongst women
                                and blessed is the
                                        fruit of thy womb

        now I am saying it
                with my brother
                        our hands across
                                our mother's body
                                        struggling to die
                                or live

        for three days
        we pray to the mother
words I have not said
        for decades

                when the time comes
                        and my brothers
                                the singers cannot
                        sing I sing to her
                in latin I thought I'd forgotten

                Ave Maria
        gratia plena

Maria gratia plena
Maria gratia plena
Ave Ave dominus
dominus tecum
benedicta
tu in mulieribus
et benedictus
et benedictus
fructus ventris
ventris tui

now I pray
Ave Cecilia
gratia plena
benedicta tu
you are blessed
and blessed
is the fruit
of your womb
we are all
blessed

Grandmother Woodchuck as St. Ann

In the stories
she is busy
making things
smoking her pipe
like any grandmother

in church
she is wearing
red and black
she is God's grandmother

when he picks up his cross
she says
why are you always
doing things like this?

he thinks if he
dies enough times
it will all come out right

she is busy
weaving
his seamless garment

Jewel Box

my mother hated books
sputtered as she
picked them up
from tables
the arms of chairs
stuffed them in the bathroom
bookcase or lost them
in the attic eaves
my mother hated books
she left me a library of jewels
I am a reader so I read them
I have no choice, it is what I do
each piece a story I hold
in my hands

there is jewelry everywhere
not just in the wooden box
on her dresser that holds
costume jewelry, summer
necklaces, her social security
card, two letters I'd written her
after her sister's death
and a birthday card from a grandchild
I feel like a child trespassing
I can't help myself
I am going where I'm not allowed

there are boxes in the top dresser drawers
a red velvet box for rings, the amethyst,
the opals, huge pink and yellow stones,
marcasite, more amethysts, rubies
on gold bands, on silver bands, on cheap
bands that would turn my fingers green
they are all in here together, but that

is not the end of it. A white hand
rises from the highboy, rings on each
finger, rings in special boxes,
here a diamond, another, here
a square emerald in a green box,
an unset sapphire in blue velvet

at the kitchen sink, a tiny glass bowl
holds more rings, peridot and coral
and another diamond
blue topaz, aquamarine,
a heart of garnets
I have no way to know
which of these are real
which are paste or glass
she wore them all

once, going somewhere special
without fancy jewelry of my own
she let me wear a necklace taking it
carefully from its box
the amethyst shone amidst
a ring of diamonds
you have to be careful with this
she said as she placed it
reverently
around my neck
all night I felt elegant
blessed by her trust
at forty finally big girl enough
to wear Mama's jewelry
but when I bring the necklace
to the jeweler
he will tell me
it's not real

pearl necklaces are in the next drawer
long and short strings, white, cream,
black, and pink fresh-water strands
some have peeling paint, but others,
who knows? I test them against my
teeth, isn't that what you do?
finally collect them all in one
satin case

onyx, jade, coral, and then
the watches, box after box, unopened,
unworn, home shopping club
in a small white stamp on the back corner
watches with jeweled bands, with
abalone faces, one white and golden
orb to wear on a necklace
its face hidden
in décolletage
like me, my mother couldn't
wear a watch
time got confused
speeded up, slowed down
she was always late
believed, we joked, in instantaneous travel
yet she has these talismans of time
time so irrelevant, ornament so irresistible

here's a see-through plastic box
molded into sections
like slices of pizza
each slice studded with earrings
big fat clip-ons, dangly
chandeliers, shining
leaves of mother-of-pearl

big gold hoops like onions
little green fish and sunbursts
next to the bed is a jewelry stand
with necklaces, silver chains
of every size, and the rosaries
her special childhood blue beads,
the white mother-of-pearl ones
that were once mine
her mother's black wooden beads
each a carved rose

here are the children's gifts
the mother pins we chose
so carefully at the five-and-ten
the rickrack earrings I made for mother's day
in second grade, a cross with no jesus
just stones in every color along its length,
the discotheque necklace my brothers bought

I carry the boxes and bags out to the car
they fill the trunk as well as books
they are bright with stories
and charged with your life, Mama
I will read them, take you home

Dressing Up

Who says redheads can't wear purple?
my mother said, pulling
another lavender sweater
over her head
do you think it's too
flamboyant?
she'd ask with a giggle
and lifted eyebrow
I never knew
how she wanted me to answer that
this fur-blend fifties
sweater-girl whose neckline
never dipped below
her collar bone
who wore high heels or
sneakers nothing
in-between
who sneered at
cabled sweaters
and tweed skirts
no Frenchwoman
would be caught dead
in those clothes
she'd announce
as she sat at the kitchen table
where she rolled her hair
over the rat-tail comb
while babies crawled
around her feet

she wore sequins
to the weekly dances
beaded sweaters bowling
and finally

for my son's wedding
I gave in and wore
a dress of black and silver
sequins and beads

we shopped together for that day
and everything was on sale
I won't tell you where
but it was not Newbury St.
when I listened to her
and bought the dress
and a drapey velvet jacket
we never broke a hundred dollars

these are the gifts we don't expect
the things we learn only later
not to scorn: the working class elegance
the unabashed love of adornment and color
and yes, these frail and beautiful bodies
our spirits comes wearing

Piano Dream

I carefully lift the lid
pour molasses
across the hammers
paint the strings
black sweet
and sulfurous
like the blues
she'll never play again
her notes
gummed
like an old woman's
joints

I kneel between
her legs open
the case draw
a heart in lipstick
on the soundboard

with chisel
and hammer I
crack it in two

Purple Ice

this story is a
violet river lit by the moon
you are wearing the silver
skates you told us about
the ones that race against
disaster and you are
skating again, no turned
ankle, no damaged hips
no promises from everyone
not to tell your daughters
you were skating in Florida
of all places up north
the lakes and ponds are
all frozen, brooks and
waterfalls caught mid-flow
and you are traveling on all
the colors of twilight this
summer I see it a path of
purple ice in the night sky
where do you skate to on this
pale river?

Figure Eight

I remember
when you showed me
how to step into infinity
how to follow the thin line as if
our two tracks were one
I traveled it over
and over
widening
that thread to a broad road
I want to believe that everything circles
back round into double curves
that when I set my foot
the ice will be lit
with faint tracings

Like a Good Death

. . . for Lisa

Lately I've dreamed of tornadoes again
and last week watched from the window
of a diner the air collect itself into
the vortex I'd kept a day ahead of
in my drive east from Albuquerque
it was the sharp edge of a storm
clouds moving rapidly south
and behind them, clouds
moving north
it took me a moment
to recognize
rotation

just before touching earth
the cloud breaks up
the swirling spirits of air
dispersed by the cold Nashaway land
well on its way
to autumn

not all beings find the cold
invigorating as those of us born to it do
our bodies burst into flame
along with the trees who are
our relatives

it is all bright colors and passion
until we drop all pretense
and stand naked
hoping someone will notice
beauty

like a good death
when we drop our flesh
bodies fall away and our spirits reveal
the beautiful and terrifying shape
of our journey through this
and all the worlds

the colors
must be
dazzling

Into Green

Peridot

it is a pear
or a green drop of dew
glittering in cold morning
sun it is the tender green
with the strength to crack
boulders it is the far-seeing
green it is sunlight
in a leafy glade

little green
the first leaf buds
shoots in snow water
this is the color
the dead see
from within the cauldron
when they are stirred
into new life

the stone is biaxial
it cleaves in two
like my mother
and myself

House of Blue Lights

From the icy
winter of the living room
to the azure of the bedroom
the kitchen a skyscape
shades of violet in the hall
and the bath of mediterranean tiles
around the resurfaced tub
there seemed no limit
every room was a blue room
in this house that was a bright
aqua beacon on the wooded road

My parents danced
in front of the stove
in the small kitchen
my father singing
my mother's hips
swinging

you'll be sure to see some sights
at the house the house
of blue lights

for awhile every
dress my mother wore
every sweater, was some shade
of water or fair sky
blue is the best color she said
as she watered plants and children
carried the weight of my grandfather
drunk again, down the stairs
while Daddy studied in night school
and my grandmother stared into
the blue light of the tv screen
til the old man was put to bed

you'll be sure to see some sights
at the house the house
of blue lights

I thought there was something
wrong with me, with my love of
autumn reds oranges and yellows
of spring greens and chocolate mud
not this constant blue blue blue
I thought she was crazy, but now
I see how she lived within this calm sea

she washed gramma's shrunken body
plunged the hypodermic into oranges
then the morphine, a daughter's duty

yes, you're sure to see some sights
in this house, this house of blue lights

For the Boy Standing Under the Drainpipe

. . . for Bill

He is wearing a fisherman's raincoat
a floppy rainhat with a long back brim
or he is not he is the boy standing under
the drainpipe in the full gushing
waterfall his eyes are closed
his head lifted into the full flow
or they are open wide under the
protective brim of his hat watching
the heavy streams enfold him he is
the boy standing under the drainpipe
and I am the girl watching he is
always there in spite of teachers
principals trips to the office it
rains and he finds the way to where
water falls dirty from the roof muddy
water plays over him where he
stands with hands outstretched or
by his sides where he spins or stands
still or circles slowly it is all he hears
the gushing voice of water the staccato
notes on shoulder and chest it is
the flowing the streaming
the warm or icy notes
their embrace

Waiting for Feathers

they were always blue
Ma's parakeets
always male

ready to bite your lip
peck at your glasses
chatter to the piano

or the voice of
johnny most announcing
a celtics game

we waited for them to appear
black and deep violet
the necklace of feathered jewels

pretty boy
we all said
pretty boy

my father called them
the family jewels
laughed

as the bird
perched on his
finger

later
when I knew
the phrase

referred to something
else something
to do with

young men
I waited and watched
eager

for the exalted plumage

Convent School

because I hate the crowded halls
I duck into the quiet chapel
where there's only a few of us
genuflecting, kneeling
in the filtered sunlight

I think I am
getting away with something
I am not saying words
I am just breathing in the silence

I don't know yet
that this is prayer

Underage

I am underage at the Twin Pines Tavern.
It's Monday night
and we're regulars here. The strobe
is flashing on my day-glo face
day-glo vines crawling up my legs,
the white satin nehru shirt
I'm wearing as a dress
luminous under black light.
I won't be in school tomorrow
or any Tuesday because after
the gig, we'll be lugging equipment
out to the van, driving the hour home
hanging out til three. I make more
in one night here than in a week
at my after-school job. Tomorrow
I'll sleep late, practice new tunes,
try to caress notes like Gracie, Aretha, Janis
summertime time time
I'm drinking Southern Comfort
between sets, *and the livin's eeeeasy*
it burns so sweet and what I don't sweat out
I burn off singing. I'm in love with Mec
every night we sing, his rough voice
soars where I want to follow. The notes
are the hands we use to touch
each other - there is nothing between us
except this music and right now that's enough
gimme some a-loving, oh lord, please
sing it again, sing it again
this bar is full of soldiers
who aren't in Nam yet I will sing

any damn thing they want
cuz you make me feel, you make me feel
hold on I'm comin, you really got a hold
on me, don't you need somebody to love?
next week I'll sing White Rabbit
til I'm sick of its *feed your head,*
feed your head, but tonight I'm
letting the good times roll,
walking the dog, getting some respect

Onyx Necklace with Pearls

the black beads
are made of velvet
they are all midnight
and musk a black cat
rubbing against her calf
now and then
she notices a light
she can let herself fall
there will be a way back

You Bring Out the Butch in Me

. . . for Diane

I want to lift weights, display my arms, throw out underwires and wear a white-ribbed tank tee-shirt. I want to carry a wrench, drive a truck, cover you with roses. I want to order artichokes in lemon and watch the olive oil darken your lips. I want to wear a velvet jacket and eye the heart-shaped ruby pendant nestled between your breasts. I want to look at you look at you look at you. I want to know you in the biblical sense. I want to watch you put on lipstick. I want to open doors, do all the driving, walk on the outside of sidewalks. I want to wear leather, strut in Doc Marten's, twirl you around a dance floor. I want you to know when I love you, that you've been loved.

Marinade

tonight you are pomegranate
and rosewater
I want to climb inside
and marinate
til morning
when I am done you
can lick sweet juices
grill me over a hot flame
I won't mind

Deep Winter

I wanted to kiss your neck
in the middle of traffic
but instead I just brushed your cheek
we'd been eating Greek food
avgolemono, moussaka, hot
flatbreads with olive oil and feta
I wanted to kiss you then
in falling snow, bring on
an early thaw

Wedding in a Burning Building

He is opposed to fire, spends his life
quelling the flames. She obeys
all the rules, sees that others do. He learns
which windows to break, which to leave alone.
She examines what has been broken, takes
down the facts.

She learns the proper procedure for firing
a gun. He learns the rules of combustion.
She learns to talk with authority. He fills
long hours with cheap conversation. She learns to flip
a man over her shoulder, to break unsuspecting bones.

He crawls under smoke, tests the walls and doors
for heat. He learns the trick of balancing on ladders. She
learns to be equally brusque with victims and muggers.
He learns to ignore the ones dead already in their beds,
looking for the one that might be saved. She covers
her heart with a properly polished badge.

The building is burning. No matter.
They are enough to fill each other's arms.

Into Green

i

I forgot
I could just sit
and lift my nose
into the warm wind

ii

I love this cloudy day
this damp air
it is cold and I am
awake

iii

above the clematis
young sparrows chirp
a heartbeat
next to the pond

iv

someone
has dragged the corncobs
out of the compost

v

I am sitting between two skies
and the voices of bullfrogs

vi

in full sun
the fish gleams ivory
and dappled shade
what joy in leaping!

vii

all day wind saunters through
pond rises to meet her

viii

after the storm
stillness
and heron's careful walk

ix

rain, lightly
I can see but cannot hear
the polyrhythms of the pond

x

during the night
pond has crept
closer to shore

xi

I've never seen a crow
bathe before, except in
dust, but here,
daintily
between the rocks
she wades in
and raises a mist

xii

so I don't get too
self-important
catbird scolds me
from the bushes
remember those
blueberries? she says
they were mine

xiii

mosquitoes mosquitoes
night after itchy night
afternoons
are jeweled with
dragonflies

xiv

in the hole in the ice
otter has been fishing
the slime on her face
is another sun

Summer Language Lesson

I am listening in
on a conversation that
I don't understand

Lightning speaking with fireflies

How to Get There

. . . for Lisa and Rick

the way must be felt
as through a dark woods
where the mossy damp
leads to a steady star
do not be deterred by thorns
the plants that wield them
often bear edible fruit
and flowers that stop your breath
with their beauty
there will be storms
learn to love them when you can
or else find the still point
there's always a fallen pine
sleeping boulders you can
crawl beneath and who
knows what friends
will shelter with you there
if you congratulate yourself
on your lack of scars
you've found a false road
go back into the bush
when lightning has filled you
enough times that you know
you will either be turned to black char
or begin to glow from within
you will find yourself in a clearing
breathe in the moist air
trees and mountains
and milky night sky
be patient
you will be found

Gamebag Dream

Grey Fox in the snow beneath my window. Wolves in the towns of Massachusetts. Eagles in the Quabbin. Black Bears at back-porch birdfeeders in the Connecticut River Valley. Snow Owls at Logan Airport. Sea Turtles at Cape Cod. Moose running through the streets of Boston. Coyotes singing in every wood.

You open the bag and the world is restored.

Aquamarine

this is the sweet color of home
the robes and nightgowns
my mother wore, the color
she painted the house
she and my father built

this stone the color of sea
holds the scent of her
after dancing
her perfume on the night air
stronger than cedar
when I open the chest

aquamarine
it is the color
of ecstatic light
the color
of something like joy

Heart

in the cottage
surrounded by rivers
a woman is sweeping
a bird flies
from window to window
never staying in
never staying out

Grandmother Knits

It begins with
swirling river blues
greens of moss wet on a log
red leaves and black nights
It begins with the fur we have lost
the softness of lamb's wool
rabbit fur on a childhood muff
and grows through encounters with
llamas on a rocky hillside
guarding a flock

It begins with two sticks
with hands moving in old
patterns passed woman
to woman like songs
that come to our lips
unbidden when the baby
cries in our arms

I will knit a vest of feathers
a house of pine cones
a shawl of maple leaves
Here is a cape of birch bark
hats of ghost elms
moccasins of pine needles

I will knit a dress of fall grass
a coat of loon calls
I will knit a nightgown of lichens
gathered from fallen logs
I will knit lace of maple syrup
I will knit a shield of raspberry canes
though my fingers will bleed

I will knit a spider web beaded with
blueberries I will knit a bed of corn silk
I will knit prayers of smoke I will knit coverlets of
cricket song pillows of milkweed down
scarves from the long howls of coyotes
I will knit embraces of warm spring rains
sweaters of squash blossoms I will knit
whatever we need my fingers
will never be still

Before Moving on to Plymouth from Cape Cod. In William Cronon's book, *Changes in the Land,* he mentions this bit of information in passing, which is often how details of colonial history get lost in cultural assumptions. I look at a sentence like this and say, they did what? Who are these people?

Bostoniak. The Abenaki word for Americans.

Entangled. Quantum mechanics suggests the concept of entangled atoms, in which the properties of one atom instantaneously affect the properties of its mate, even when the two are physically separated by substantial distances. Einstein called this "spooky action at a distance." We call it knowing things.

Daughters of the King. From "Daughters of the King." The American Canadian Genealogist, Vol. 21, No 1. Issue 64. Winter, 1995.

Grandmother Woodchuck. The grandmother of Gluscabe who appears in many of our traditional stories. For more about her see Joseph Bruchac, *The Wind Eagle and Other Abenaki Stories,* Bowman Books.

Indian Blood. Type O blood, a common blood type all over the world, gives some resistance to smallpox. This resulted in a large proportion of the Northeast Native population having this blood type as they were the ones who survived the epidemics. For a long time, scientists did not make this connection, and it was mistakenly asserted that Indian people did not share the same blood types as the rest of the world.

Red. In our creation stories, human beings are created from trees. The last lines of the poem are a quote from Chrystos.

Smallpox. The information on smallpox is from Jennifer Lee Carrell, *The Speckled Monster,* Plume Penguin, 2004. In Boston, in 1720, 500 people were inoculated against smallpox, and by the end of the 1700's, vaccinations with the less dangerous vaccinia virus began. Jeffrey Amherst wrote his famous letters advocating the use of smallpox blankets to eradicate Indians in 1763. Thanks also to Lisa Clark, microbiologist for her help with this poem.

Surrogate mothers. During behavioral experiments in the 1950's and 1960's, monkey infants were taken from their mothers and placed with cylindrical wire cages covered with cloth. These cages were called "surrogate mothers," as they were supposed to replace the monkeys' natural mothers. In fact, the infant monkeys clung to the surrogate mothers, preferring their touch to none at all. During the 1980's, the term "surrogate mother" was appropriated to describe natural birth mothers whose children were conceived as part of a sales agreement. When the mothers bore their children and decided not to sell them, the media used this term to imply that the actual birth mother was, in fact, only a surrogate.

Newfoundland. At the same time that there were bounties on the heads of Indian people in Maine, there was an attempt to exterminate Newfoundlands, who were Indian dogs. In his journal, Joseph Brant mentions a Newfoundland who traveled with him out to Ohio.

Acknowledgements

"At Sugarloaf" appeared in an earlier form in *The Eye of the Deer*, edited by Carolyn Dunn and Carol Comfort, Aunt Lute Books, 1999.

"Red" appeared in *Gatherings*, Fall, 1998.

"Rosary," "The Willow at Flint Pond," and "Hurricane–North Truro" appeared in earlier forms *French Connections: A Gathering of Franco-American Poets*, edited by Christine Gelineau, Louisiana Literature Press, 2006.

"No Pity" and "Underage" appeared in *Peregrine*, Fall, 1999.

"Les Filles du Roi" appeared in *Potato Eyes*, Spring, 1997.

"Heart" appeared in *Sojourner*, 1991.